Prolance

www.prolancewriting.com
California, USA
©2017 Hosai Mojaddidi
Illustrations ©2017 Teresa Abboud

ISBN: 978-0-9983287-8-2

Clear the Path

A Rhyme Book on Manners for Little Muslims

Written by Hosai Mojaddidi
Illustrated by Teresa Abboud

PROLANCE

Dedication

Glory be to God, the Exalted, who through His Grace and Mercy, has blessed us with an intimate knowledge of His Beloved, the Prophet Muhammad ﷺ (God's peace and blessings upon him), the greatest teacher who ever lived. I sincerely pray that whoever reads this book grows in their love and understanding of his beautiful and exquisite character. I pray that every parent and every child, every teacher and every student study the meanings deeply and bring his perfect example to life through their own actions and words.

To my loving husband, Haider, and my precious sons, Yasin and Ismail, you are the greatest treasures of my life. You fill my days with laughter and light, and because of that, I am inspired to write. To my beloved parents, Mohammed and Aqelah, and my incredible siblings, Malalai, Haroon, Wazhma, and Tariq, thank you for your continued love, support, and encouragement over the years. You have always believed in me and pushed me to be my best.

To my esteemed teacher, Shaykh Hamza Yusuf, I credit you solely for introducing me to who the Prophet ﷺ actually is and what it truly means to love him. Thank you for your invaluable guidance and wisdom, and for never hesitating to share your genuine love of the Beloved ﷺ with the world.

To all my family, dear friends, and supporters, near and far, hidden and known, thank you for inspiring me every day.

I am a Muslim; I say the truth.
I mind my manners, yes I do.

I say *salam* before I speak.
I love Allah: His happiness I seek.

I shake hands, so my sins will fall.
I turn around when my name is called.

I take my shoes off: no tracking dirt.
I clear the path, so no one gets hurt.

I say "*bismillah*" before I eat and drink.
I rinse my hands and then dry the sink.

I am a Muslim; I say the truth.
I mind my manners, yes I do.

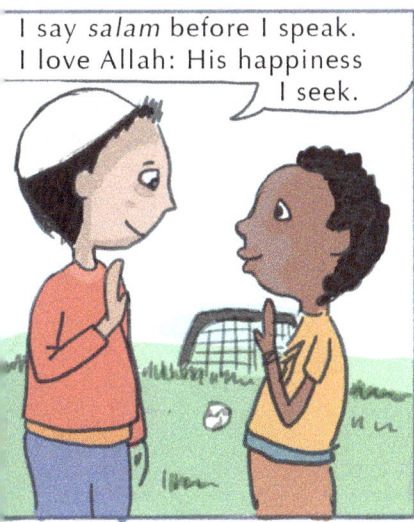

I say *salam* before I speak.
I love Allah: His happiness
I seek.

I shake hands, so my sins
will fall.

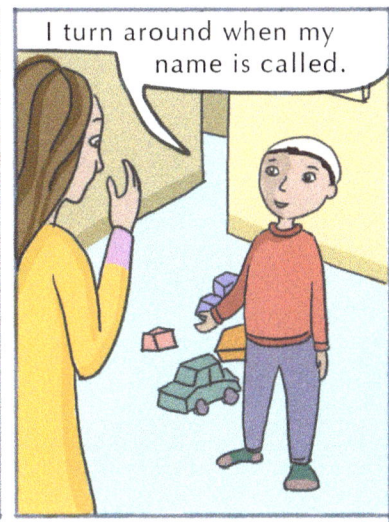

I turn around when my
name is called.

I take my shoes off: no tracking dirt.
I clear the path, so no one gets hurt.

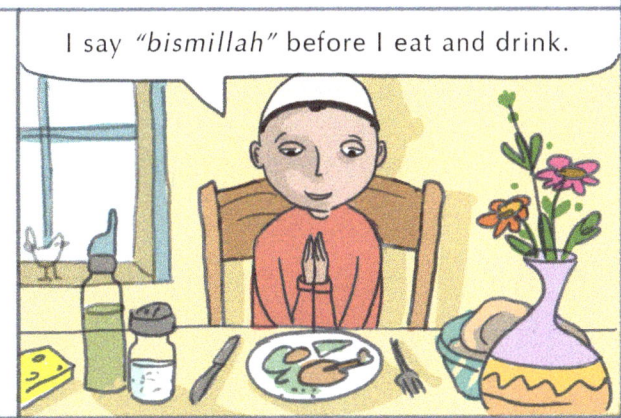

I say *"bismillah"* before I eat and drink.

I rinse my hands and then dry the sink.

I am a Muslim; I say the truth.
I mind my manners, yes I do.

I never frown or whine when I don't get my way.
I speak my mind when I have nice things to say.

I trust good people who I know don't lie.
I'm not suspicious and will never spy or pry.

I pay attention and don't interrupt.
I remain quiet and never say "shut up."

I praise Allah when I feel grateful and glad.
I praise Allah when I feel upset and sad.

Sharing & Caring

I am a Muslim; I say the truth.
I mind my manners, yes I do.

I save my money to help people in need.
I give my time to increase my good deeds.

I share my food and offer the best thing first.
I drink three small sips to quench my thirst.

I visit the sick to help ease their pain.
I pray their strength and health will remain.

I sit with my elders and ask them how they are.
I help them walk to and from the car.

Cleaning & Dressing

I am a Muslim; I say the truth.
I mind my manners, yes I do.

I brush my hair back and keep it in place.
I wash my hands and scrub clean my face.

I brush my teeth, so they're shiny and white.
I floss before I sleep every single night.

I keep the things in my room looking nice and neat.
I make my own bed and dust clean the sheets.

I hang my clothes and fold my socks in a ball.
I put my books away and never write on the wall.

I am a Muslim; I say the truth. I mind my manners, yes I do.

I brush my hair back and keep it in place.

I wash my hands and scrub clean my face.

I brush my teeth, so they're shiny and white.

I floss before I sleep every single night.

I keep the things in my room looking nice and neat.

I make my own bed and dust clean the sheets.

I put my books away and never write on the wall.

I hang my clothes and fold my socks in a ball.

I am a Muslim; I say the truth.
I mind my manners, yes I do.

I make fresh *wudu* and then say my *du'as.*
I lay my prayer mat out and stand in pause.

I face the qibla and say, "Allah is Great!"
I don't move around and keep my body straight.

I bow and rise, as my eyes stay cast down.
I press my forehead gently onto the ground.

I say *salams* and face left and right.
I love praying to Allah day and night.

I am a Muslim; I say the truth.
I love my *deen,* and so should you!

am a Muslim; I say the truth.
mind my manners, yes I do.

I make fresh *wudu* and then say my *du'as*.

I lay my prayer mat out and stand in pause.

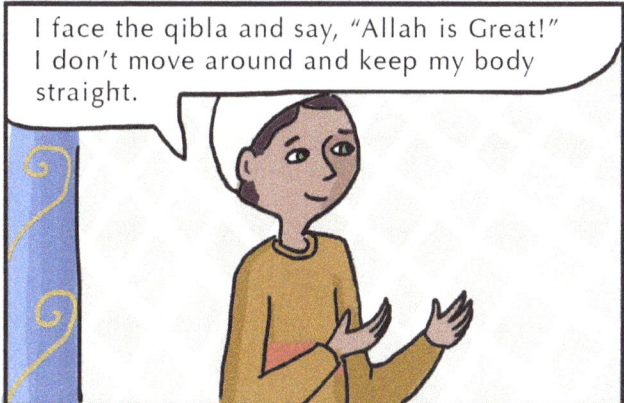

I face the qibla and say, "Allah is Great!" I don't move around and keep my body straight.

I bow and rise, as my eyes stay cast down. I press my forehead gently onto the ground.

I say *salams* and face left and right. I love praying to Allah day and night.

I am a Muslim; I say the truth. I love my *deen,* and so should you!

Related Hadiths
for Parents & Educators
Greeting & Visiting

According to a sound hadith, the Prophet Muhammad ﷺ said, "I have been sent to perfect noble character." To honor his excellent example, the verses in this book are all based on sound traditions from his blessed life. The following section provides references for every verse, in sequential order, so that you may explain to your children and/or students the significance of each act and encourage them to follow in the footsteps of the Beloved of God ﷺ.

The Prophet Muhammad ﷺ said, "Truthfulness leads to righteousness, and righteousness leads to Paradise." (Al-Bukhari)

The Prophet Muhammad ﷺ said, "The person nearest to God, the Exalted, is the one who is first to offer the greeting." (Abu Dawud)

The Prophet Muhammad ﷺ said, "There are no two Muslims who meet and shake hands with one another except that they will be forgiven before they part." (Abu Dawud)

Ali ibn Abi Talib (may God be pleased with him) said about the Prophet ﷺ, "When he would turn, he would turn to face one with his whole body." (At-Tirmidhi)

The Prophet Muhammad ﷺ said, "When you put on your shoes, begin with the right, and, when removing them, begin with the left so that the right shoe is the first to be put on and the last to be taken off." (Muslim)

The Prophet Muhammad ﷺ said, "Removing a harmful thing from the path is a charitable act." (Al-Bukhari)

The Prophet Muhammad ﷺ said, "Mention God's name before you start eating; eat with your right hand; and eat from what is near you." (Al-Bukhari)

The Prophet Muhammad ﷺ said, "Cleanliness is half of faith." (Muslim)

The Prophet Muhammad ﷺ said, "The blessing of food is in washing before and after the meal." (Imam Ahmad)

Related Hadiths
for Parents & Educators
Listening & Speaking

The Prophet Muhammad ﷺ said, "Truthfulness leads to righteousness, and righteousness leads to Paradise." (Al-Bukhari)

Abu Hurairah (may God be pleased with him) said, "A man said to the Prophet ﷺ 'Give me advice.' The Prophet ﷺ said, 'Do not get angry.' The man asked repeatedly [for more advice], and the Prophet ﷺ answered each time, 'Do not get angry.'" (Al-Bukhari)

The Prophet Muhammad ﷺ said, "Hearts naturally love those who are kind to them and loathe those who are cruel." (Al-Bayhaqi)

The Prophet Muhammad ﷺ said, "A believer cannot be a liar." (Imam Malik)

The Prophet Muhammad ﷺ said, "Beware of suspicion: suspicion is the falsest kind of speech; do not spy or pry." (Al-Bukhari)

The Prophet Muhammad ﷺ said, "Beware of suspicion, for it is the most deceitful of thought." (Al-Bukhari & Muslim)

Aisha (may God be pleased with her) said about the Prophet ﷺ, "When he spoke, one could count his words if one wished to." (Al-Bukhari)

The Prophet Muhammad ﷺ said, "Do not say anything for which you will have to say you are sorry." (Ibn Majah)

The Prophet Muhammad ﷺ said, "May God have mercy on a servant who spoke well and gained good, or kept silent and avoided harm." (Ibn al-Mubarak)

The Prophet Muhammad ﷺ said, "How wondrous is the case of a believer; there is good for him in everything, and this applies only to a believer. If prosperity befalls him, he expresses gratitude to God, and that is good for him; and if adversity befalls him, he endures it patiently, and that is good for him." (Muslim)

Related Hadiths
for Parents & Educators
Sharing & Caring

The Prophet Muhammad ﷺ said, "Truthfulness leads to righteousness, and righteousness leads to Paradise." (Al-Bukhari)

The Prophet Muhammad ﷺ said, "The upper hand is better than the lower hand (i.e., he who gives charity is better than he who takes it)." (Al-Bukhari)

The Prophet Muhammad ﷺ said, "The food of two persons suffices for three persons, and the food of three persons suffices for four persons." (Al-Bukhari)

The Prophet Muhammad ﷺ said, "When any of you takes a meal, let him eat, receive, and share it with the right hand." (Al-Bukhari & Muslim)

The Prophet Muhammad ﷺ said, "Love for humanity what you love for yourself." (Al-Bukhari)

The Prophet Muhammad ﷺ said, "Visit the sick, feed the hungry, and free the one who is imprisoned [unjustly]." (Al-Bukhari)

The Prophet Muhammad ﷺ said, "The most rewarding visitation of the sick is the one that is appropriately brief." (Ad-Daylami)

The Prophet Muhammad ﷺ said, "The young should greet the elderly." (Al-Bukhari)

The Prophet Muhammad ﷺ said, "A young man never honors an old man due to his age but that God sends someone to honor him when he reaches that age." (At-Tirmidhi)

The Prophet Muhammad ﷺ said, "Whoever fails to care for our youth, respect our aged, enjoin right, and denounce wrong is not counted among us." (Imam Ahmad)

Aisha (may God be pleased with her) said about the Prophet Muhammad ﷺ, "There was no one with a better character than the Messenger of God ﷺ. Whenever any of his Companions or the people of his household called him, he would reply, 'At your service!'" (An-Nasa'i)

The Prophet Muhammad ﷺ said, "It is the sunnah for a man to go out with his guest to the door of the house." (Ibn Majah)

Related Hadiths
for Parents & Educators
Cleaning & Dressing

The Prophet Muhammad ﷺ said, "Truthfulness leads to righteousness, and righteousness leads to Paradise." (Al-Bukhari)

Aisha (may God be pleased with her) said, "The Prophet Muhammad ﷺ used to like starting from the right in performing *wudu*, in combing his hair, and in putting on his shoes." (Al-Bukhari)

The Prophet Muhammad ﷺ said, "I have told you repeatedly to use the *siwak* (toothbrush)." (Al-Bukhari)

Hudhaifah (may God be pleased with him) said, "When the Prophet Muhammad ﷺ got up at night, he would brush his teeth with the *siwak*." (An-Nasa'i)

The Prophet Muhammad ﷺ said, "When you intend going to bed at night, put out the lights, close the doors, tie the mouths of the water skins, and cover your food and drinks." (Al-Bukhari)

The Prophet Muhammad ﷺ said, "God loves a servant who when performing a task does so skillfully." (Al-Bayhaqi)

The Prophet Muhammad ﷺ said, "When any of you goes to his bed, he should dust his bedding with his waist cloth, for he does not know what has come on it since he left it." (Al-Bukhari)

Umm Salamah (may God be pleased with her) said, "The clothing which the Messenger of God ﷺ liked best was the shirt." (Abu Dawud)

The Prophet Muhammad ﷺ said, "God is Beautiful and loves beauty." (Muslim)

The Prophet Muhammad ﷺ said, "Stay clean as best you can, for God established Islam upon cleanliness." (Ar-Rafi'i)

Related Hadiths
for Parents & Educators
Praying & Supplicating

Suggested resources for studying *seerah*:

"Life of the Prophet Muhammad" by Shaykh Hamza Yusuf (CD set)
The Content of Character: Ethical Sayings of the Prophet Muhammad by Shaykh Hamza Yusuf
Muhammad: His Life Based on the Earliest Sources by Martin Lings

The Prophet Muhammad ﷺ said, "Truthfulness leads to righteousness, and righteousness leads to Paradise." (Al-Bukhari)

The Prophet Muhammad ﷺ said, "There is no *salat* for one who does not have *wudu*, and there is no *wudu* for one who does not mention the name of God." (Ibn Majah)

Aisha (may God be pleased with her) said, "The Messenger of God ﷺ had a reed mat that he would spread out during the day and make into a compartment at night towards which he would perform prayer." (Ibn Majah)

The Prophet Muhammad ﷺ said, "Whoever prays as we pray, turns to face the same qibla as us, and eats *zabihah* meat is a Muslim." (At-Tirmidhi)

The Prophet Muhammad ﷺ said, "The most excellent prayer is that in which the duration of *qiyam* (standing) is lengthened." (Muslim)

Amr bin Sa'd (may God be pleased with him) said, "The Messenger of God ﷺ used to say the *taslim* [greeting given when ending the prayer] to his right and to his left." (An-Nasa'i)

The Prophet Muhammad ﷺ said, "Prayer is the central pillar of religion; prayer is the key to every good." (Al-Hakim)

The Prophet Muhammad ﷺ said, "True spiritual excellence is devotion to God as if you see Him; and though you do not see Him, you at least know that He sees you." (Al-Bukhari & Muslim)

The Prophet Muhammad ﷺ said, "For whomever God wants good, He gives him understanding in the *deen* (religion)." (At-Tirmidhi)

About the Author

Hosai Mojaddidi is a former private school teacher and current homeschooling mom, writer/editor, activist, mental health advocate, and public speaker. She is the co-Founder of MH4M (www.mentalhealth4muslims.com), a content driven site that provides resources and articles on mental health related topics tailored for the Muslim community. She is passionate about teaching children Qur'an, Islamic studies, and the importance of refinement and etiquette based on the teachings and perfect life of the best of mankind, the Prophet Muhammad ﷺ.

She resides in California with her family and offers monthly spiritual wellness classes for women, educational workshops for students and teachers, and regular talks at mosques and Islamic organizations locally and nationally on a variety of subjects ranging from spiritual development, marriage/family, education, mental health in Islam, women's issues, interfaith topics, *seerah*, etc. In her spare time, she enjoys reading, writing, and blogging via social media (Facebook and Twitter), doing arts and crafts, visiting gourmet coffee shops, and exploring the countless beautiful beaches and parks throughout California.

www.ingramcontent.com/pod-product-compliance
Lightning Source LLC
Chambersburg PA
CBHW041634040426

42447CB00019B/3483